COFFEE HOUSE
CONFESSIONS

COFFEE HOUSE CONFESSIONS

Poems

Ellaraine Lockie

SILVER BIRCH PRESS

LOS ANGELES, CALIFORNIA, USA

ISBN-13: 978-0615727677

ISBN-10: 0615727670

FIRST EDITION, 2013

EMAIL: silverbirchpress@yahoo.com
WEB: silverbirchpress.com

BOOK DESIGN: Silver Birch Press
COVER PHOTO: Nick Warzin, nickwarzin.com
AUTHOR PHOTO: Shawn Lockie

ACKNOWLEDGMENTS

JAVA GENETICS: *Rattlesnake Review*

WHITE NOISE AND OTHER MUSES: *Presa*

ASHES: *Heavy Bear*; *Word Press*; *Minotaur*; *Lummox*

TAO OF TAOS: *EDGZ*; *Winning Writers*

CENSURED AT SEATTLE'S BEST: *The Centrifugal Eye*; *Waterways*; *Guerilla Poetics Project Reader*

TRAVEL WRITER: *Ibbetson Street*

THEY SPEAK STARBUCKS IN ITALY: *San Gabriel Valley Poetry Journal*

TORNA A SURRIENTO: *The Centrifugal Eye*

POETS IN PORTUGAL: *Stroking David's Leg*

THE YOUNG AND THE RESTLESS: *Ibbetson Street*

PATRIOTISM ON TRIAL: *Poesy*; *Minotaur*; *Zygote in My Coffee*

MAN ABOUT TOWN: *Guerilla Poetics Project Reader; Cyclamen and Swords*; *Empty Shoes: Poems on the Hungry and the Homeless*

SHORT-SHORTS ON MIDLIFE LEGS: *Mind's Eye Newsletter*; *Free Focus*; *The Other Herald*

IN THE PRIVACY OF PUBLIC: *Taproot Literary Review*

HERO: *Scratch*: *Scratch Anthology*

CRAZY: *Iconoclast*

SYNESTHESIA AT A POETRY READING: *Jones Av.* (Canada); *Heavy Bear; Rattlesnake Review*

MASQUERADES: *The Silt Reader*; *Free Verse*; *HazMat Literary Review*; *A Long and Winding Road*

RELATIVELY SPEAKING: *Unlikely Stories*

SINGLE AT THE SECOND CUP COFFEE SHOP: *Main Street Rag*

WHERE THERE'S SMOKE: *Presa*; *Fresh Grass*

STUCK IN THE WEB: *ESC! Magazine*; *Exit 13 Magazine*; *Song of the San Joaquin Quarterly; Chaparral Updrafts*; *California Quarterly*

WHAT'S IN A NAME: *Home Planet News*

BLESSINGS: *The Más Tequila Review*; *Mis en Poem* (France)

JUST DESERTS: *Pearl*

YOU'VE COME A LONG WAY BABY: *Chiron Review; ESC! Magazine; Medusa's Kitchen; PoetryMagazine.com*

CONTENTS

JAVA GENETICS

A gene seed planted by need
when primal people had no written words
So gathered around fires
to transfer stories face to face
And poetry sprouted out of rhymes
that stuck in slippery memories

A gene seed germinating
over generational turfs
Wrapping resolve around chromosomes
that pulled poets too poor
for heated rooms toward coffee houses
Where they huddled around brick hearths
Passed their poems on with quill pens
and recited them to kindred spirits

A gene seed congenital now in a select few
We who buy the beans in one-pound bags
Transport them home to plunge hands
into the oil slicked harvest
Inhale the redolence that rises
around a coffee grinder's clamor

Only to find the fix incomplete
Creativity dependent on the high in a coffee house
The scene a certain amphetamine
We're as homogenized as the milk in café au lait
that must be drunk in the company of like kind
An inheritance from prehistoric people
hedging fires and proliferating
a gene seed planted by need

WHITE NOISE AND OTHER MUSES

The woman sitting next to me in Starbucks says
I wish I were as dedicated to something
as you to whatever you do here every day
Little does she know I'm eating her alive
Dissecting her and spitting her out on paper
That I'm bulimic about everything
surrounding me in any public place

Here air animates like caffeine
continually pumped through lungs
The ongoing coffee grind aroma that's over
at home every morning as fast as orgasm

Music a pep pill dispersed by satellite
Set of 60s hits today; *A Hard Day's Night*
and my first boyfriend stares
at my newly swollen breasts
Wanting more than the poem I'll write
about the Catholic Church and hand jobs

He's soon swallowed by a John Cage cacophony
Staccato of espresso machine and blender
Bow of chairs scratching across belly of floor
Whoosh of milk steamer as soft as a chinook
floating a mélange of multi-voices

A sanctuary so oddly tranquil that time stands still
Senses sharpen and I cut into the lace
of sunlight that embroiders my table
Into the man outside talking to himself in a bathrobe
The rough-draft-of-a-woman sitting next to me
That earlier version of myself

ASHES

He's been to this Starbucks before
Someone at a nearby table says
he rotates to avoid arrest
A mountain man or maybe Santa Claus look
Except skinny as a stage-four Jesus
Guitar on top of his grocery cart
over piles of clothes and a bag of cat food
Cat food, when there's no place for a cat
Twenty-six degrees last night and damp

Yesterday it was a moth beating against
the outside glass
A feverish fight for survival
that I instantly knew I'd assist
But my mental clock ticks slower now
In considerations about connecting
to a man without roots
One who could become a daily complication

Minutes pass that prefer moths
before the man leaves his cart
and heads for the alley
An image of dumpster food replaces denial
of my Montana heritage
that decrees humane as religion

Mountain Man returns from the direction
of the Mobile station with a pack of Camels
Rips off the plastic and lights one up
Burning with it the sandwich I was about to buy him
and the conscience that forbade my vanilla bean scone
When I walk to the car
his head and back bend over guitar scratches
that no one would ever pay to hear

➤

11

At home I sweep up the ashes
Moths that chose flames
Salem cigarettes and Valium prescriptions
smoldering somewhere in the past
The day has disappeared in smoke

TAO OF TAOS
—After Wired? Coffee Cyber Cafe
in Taos, New Mexico

                    I
A big Teddy Bear man rakes the pebbles
of a Buddhist Zen sand garden out front
A totem pole watches while water drips
from boulders into pools in ancient rhythms
And a rock-lined creek sings a song
of renewal that gods have bowed to

You feel as though you've had Prozac even before
walking through the screened porch door
into the organic nursery that is the foyer
Behind which the open arms of contentment await
A black cat named Cosmo curled in its lap
Cubbyholes, atriums, quiet-only areas
and enclosed patios attach like limbs
dressed in glass beads, rattan and organic cotton

Ceiling fans slow-dance the soft shawl of sun
from skylights and walls of glass
across clusters of houseplants
Indoor water recycles the sound of baptism
as it bubbles from a bamboo log
into a granite pond guarded by a stone fetish
Cement glistens wet and fog breathes new life
into the air from a fountain of ceramic
                                        ➤

II

Like Taos itself, angles and levels
allow no squared-off judgments
Not with the cohabitation of these multi-cultured icons
The giftshop Buddha statue, dashboard Jesus
woodblocked Milagros, Yiddish proverbed mugs
Shiva and Freud cloth-sculptured magnets
and Saint Ann Patron of Lost Objects
All giving audience to the music of *Arabic Groove*
Italian Cafe and *Sahara Lounge*

You start to feel one with it all
as you sit and sip French roast
That you're part of what flows and glows
falls and rises, purrs and dances
That words could never wash away
the dirt of daily life
like the silence of this salvation

While gazing on the backyard garden
Verdant and blossomed with birdbath, benches
tiny temples and a mythological goat
whose belly pots a plant
A spider on the wall jumps onto your table
And you leap shriek into terror
But only think the *Damn it to hell*
that would expel you from Paradise

Recuperation is a line for the restroom
with Chinese lettering and lizards
on the ceiling that aren't alive
The Teddy Bear owner leads you to another bathroom
in the office where he counsels the depressed
the paranoid, the broken, the people who can't connect
You walk past the coffee bar blackboard
where the quote for the day reads
The most important thing about communication
is to hear what isn't being said

CENSURED AT SEATTLE'S BEST

A book bumps my
Swiss chocolate bar off the tiny table
to the freshly wiped wooden floor
Where the carefully rationed quota
of daily decadence
winks cocoa bean brown eyes
in clandestine persuasion

I'd pick it up
and plop it in my mouth
The life expectancy of most germs
being less than sixty seconds
If it weren't for the three-year-old boy
watching like a dog-in-waiting
to see what my next move might be

Role model mindful
And with meagerly concern
for castigation from customers
old enough to consume coffee
I proceed with the picking up part
and place the chocolate by my thesaurus

The implied trip
to the trash can in the corner
is obscured behind a need to write longer
than a three-year-old's attention span
and a clientele's turnover
When I can complete
my consummation of the culinary act

TRAVEL WRITER

He scans my face
as I sit at a Starbucks table
Stockbroker in a Silicon Valley suit
Finishes his cell phone services with *I love you*
Then looks up my skirt
I fix eyes colder than iced coffee
on his two faces

The old man on my left
has been trying to read my writing
for the last ten minutes
If I make eye contact
he'll ask the obligatory question
Then inundate me about his Navy days
in World War II while I continue to write
between slapdash glances in his direction

And the woman two tables to my right
with cherub cheeks and friendly demeanor
will condemn me, maybe not to hell
But surely to the Miss Manners' column
in the newspaper over which she's watching
I avert her gaze and go the distance
that my pen travels
Into the remote terrain of a writer

THEY SPEAK STARBUCKS IN ITALY

When I order
two shots of espresso
The order taker and coffee maker
at the Bar La Cisteria says
You want two espresso
holding up a demi-cup in each hand

No, two in one cup, I say
He carries both cups to the machine
No second cup I say louder
He flings arms wide enough to hold
every American word he's ever heard
Palms open to the heavens in a plea
probably for no more customers like me

In my first Italian body-talk lesson
I take a used cup from the counter top
With a sweeping flourish hold out two fingers
and poke them into the cup
His prayer slips into shoulders that shrug
You want doppio, why not say so

TORNA A SURRIENTO

Shredded edges on the stack of drafts
speak the age of the poem they portray
Coffee stains marble the top sheets
The smell as alive as the tourists
who droned *Piazza's* statue in *Tasso Square*
As strong as the magnetic pull
of our hands as we strolled

Tinkles from inlaid music boxes
stirred the air with earth essence
of handcrafted leather and *Costa D'Amalfi*
lemons in store soaps and *limoncello*
On the day you spilled Italian roast at *Il Fauno*
My shriek competing with the tenor singing Caruso
The burn on my arm abated by your hand on my thigh

That burn throbs like a heartbeat now
I file the drafts and call upon
the coffee god's gift of olfactory amnesia
How the beans are breathed
in perfumeries to replace the previous scent

Torna a Surriento: Return to Sorrento

POETS IN PORTUGAL

Sated in shellfish cataplana
queijadas* and the Cascais coastline

Energized by bullfights
where the bulls don't die

By sun-ripened skin
on women in full bloom

And on men with guitar fingers
and blazing eyes that melt language barriers

I drink espresso that floats a cinnamon stick
And push my pen across space with the ghosts

of Lord Byron, Hans Christian Andersen
and Luis Vaz de Camões

*cheesecake

PATRIOTISM ON TRIAL

In Portugal I buy a brown
leather jacket for my passport
Divorcing myself from the navy blue plastic
that announces my marriage to a country
murdering people for political purposes

In Spain I turn my San Francisco
sweatshirt inside out
Avoid long conversations with locals
In Italy I work on a Canadian accent
and don't ask for Catsup in cafes

In Mexico Sergio Witz Rodriguez
has been arrested for writing a poem
that images his country's flag as a rag
A replacement for toilet paper
Metaphors that provoke a fine and prison
in the mind of Mexico's Supreme Court

In London I read the guilty verdict
Lay *The Morning Star* on Starbuck's table
Go into the loo where I reverse my sweatshirt
And return to write a poem
over the front page print
about the felonies that stain freedom

THE YOUNG AND THE RESTLESS

The German Shepherd James Dean of Dogs
shoves his snout into the crotch of a passer-by
Then into his mistress' purse
Pulls out a pack of cigarettes that scatter the patio
of the Solid Grounds Coffee House

As she plays pick-up
he uproots two petunias from a planter
Then jumps into the box and plows through
the rest of the spring flowers

Stops when his nose touches glass
and eyes meet mine on the inside
I look into the chocolate rhinestone studded eyes
of my father instead of James Dean

Hear his bedtime stories told from recall
rather than from books we couldn't afford
A boy dingle-bumping the girls
on a Montana wire fence
The turning over of outhouses
with owners inside on Halloween

Like a circus dog in one flying leap
the owner of my father's eyes
lands mostly in his mistress' lap
Blueberry Rooibus, queen tea of the day
reigns over the table and cobblestone
His tongue over her face

Through surreal of slobber on glass
my grandmother gasps when she finds
a quarter horse turned loose in her sitting room
And eating apples from a hand-painted porcelain bowl
that came to America on the boat with her

➤

The woman ties her charge to the table legs
while she comes inside to collect napkins
The dog watches her until she disappears
He sniffs the air then yanks the table toward
leftovers in a garbage can
I can't see his eyes but they would be closed
to any interference

The boy hopes to be hidden
when he stands on Charlie Russell's shoes
Under a long trench coat as the ensemble
ambled into a girlie show
Where he will be the only ten-year-old in attendance

The mistress commands *Down*
and eases into a Danielle Steel romance
just as a man walks by with a border collie
A barker who would challenge
the James Dean in any dog
And the table disappears from under Danielle Steel
Bumps its way down the sidewalk after the dogs

A school principal with red dripping
from his face and whip in hand
yells as he chases the young father-to-be
and Skinny Cofield down an alley
After they have bounced red inkwells
off his head to avoid a whipping

The mistress is faster than the principal and now ties
the leash around her waist as she prepares to leave
Her dog licks his maleness which will no doubt
soon be sacrificed as an offering for serenity
A fate that didn't await my father
Cause for a double Caramel Cream Frappaccino

Man About Town

His stride was a study in meter
And any female looking his way
from the Leaf and Bean
as he crossed the street
would become an immediate student

Black leather blazer
Body cigar-straight in blue jeans
tucked into boots
Dark hair growing out of his halfway
unbuttoned tan shirt
Two-day stubble and longhair look
of a GQ model

Five sips of coffee later I look up
And he's ransacking
the four trash cans out front
Toasting other people's excess
with paper cups
In moves as fluid as the lattes
chai and chocolate milks
that slide down his throat

He's become a fine wine connoisseur
Who couldn't be bothered to replace
hiking boots with soles wallet-thin
Whose domestic help forgot to hem
the lining that hangs below black leather
Or wash the once-white shirt
that wears the foods he's scavenging
➤

Now he's the city sanitation engineer
conducting a field study
Who sets aside samples of pizza
submarine sandwiches and chicken wing bones
 Scoops it all with bureaucratic certainty
into a threadbare backpack
And not one of us watching
wishes to humble him
with the truth of a hand-out

SHORT-SHORTS ON MIDLIFE LEGS

Does she know
how the back of her thighs
look without shadow of shade

That sunrays ripple
bumpy waves beneath skin surface
Flab surplus slapping
the shore of her shorts
As she settles into Peet's
sidewalk table

I suspect she does
but doesn't care
Her mind on more weighty
matters than her ample pounds

Like the library stack of books
on bird migration she carries
And the Cafe Mocha
she consumes with them
Never once looking up
for approval from other eyes

Autonomy entitling her
to head my heroine list
Above even Meryl Streep
Who bears soul beyond body
beneath brightest screen lights
But she doesn't disclose cellulite

IN THE PRIVACY OF PUBLIC

Two women sit silent
surrounded by the clamor of the coffee shop
Matching shades of sandy blonde hair
The same sea-green eyes
Except the younger pair
stare through rims red as coral
into some far-off horizon
The light in them drowned

Beacons in the older set
Her hand stretched
across the table stroking the other woman's
folded arm that holds up her chin
Only one blink when saltwater eyes
are dabbed with a napkin

The ice in one glass has melted
Coffee across from it would be cold
Yet the rubbing does not ebb
Something horrible here that can be alluded to
only through an umbilical cord
And perhaps only in the privacy of public

HERO

The man practically salutes
as he steps into Starbucks dressed in khaki
Sleeves emblazoned by three gold stripes
His background written as though
it were a big print history book
across the military mustache
Across hair mowed like the grey bristle of a brush
Perfect posture in spite of the cane
Pride flashing like a bronze medal in the sun

Yet he's allowed the young woman wearing
a convalescent home badge to open the door
He says something in a slurred stew of words
She holds out an Etch-a-Sketch
When she can read the word *toilet*
he rewards her with a smile cut in horizontal half
A pat on her shoulder
before he hobbles to independence
Fantasies of him as my parent crowd images
of an angry mother demanding to be spoon fed
and coddled like a hand-blown egg by her daughter

The vet refuses the wheelchair table
Sits alone with a newspaper for company
A napkin tucked into his shirt neck
Another in his good hand to wipe coffee
and cake crumbs that don't hit their target
He thumbs-up the aide when she says *Fifteen minutes*
before she joins her chain-smoking charges
at an outside table
Like a Basset Hound on the scent of time
he begins to audit each of his watches
One on each wrist
➤

And I want to join the ranks of
my mother's neighbors, friends and paid strangers
People important enough to impress
Today's hero couldn't shout
I changed your diapers even if he wanted to

CRAZY

*Two observers cannot see the same rainbow. Each
eye sees its own.*
   —The National Center for Atmospheric Research

They call her crazy at the coffee shop
Not while she sits sipping
from a whipped cream topped cup
Her out of the blue tongue-rolling trills
as surprising as the local flock of wild parrots
if they flew in for a coffee break

Except the parrots wouldn't be clapping hands
to piped-in Bob Dylan songs, slapping legs
snapping fingers or smiling their hearts inside out
Nor would they suddenly say
Bless you WOO in falsetto
when someone across the room sneezes

I order a refill and ask about her
A woman who comes in several times a day carrying
a recycled paper cup until it protests into pieces
Arms extended from body like wings
Always wearing polyester in pastels
that dress any day in a rainbow

Other customers don't look at her
or at the definition of Tourette syndrome
I peek over the poem I'm writing about birds
Pretend I'm watching people on the sidewalk
She feigns nothing when she hawk-eyes children
like she might pick them up
and take them back to her nest for playtime
                                    ➤

Instead she baby-steps out the door
a certain stilted rhythm in her stride
And says *Thank you very MUCH*
to whatever god guides her
No one calls her crazy until after she leaves

I return to the birds that sing
flutter and feed from my fig tree
Oblivious of the cat still as a garden statue
under the lowest branch
But I'll wait for this woman every morning

For the call of the wild that frees
a coffee house from its cage
For the cleansing flush of a rainbow
Its antidote for impending storms

SYNESTHESIA AT A POETRY READING

He reads wearing blue Bermuda shorts
at a Border's coffee shop
for a small but rapt audience
The front tables filled with females
There to increase their appreciation of poetry
and its effect on scrambling the senses
For which the poet is infamous

They listen with eyes that grow large
Then bigger as words bulge
into about nine inches of metaphor
escaping from his mouth
A meaty tone that wants to burst through blue
They see through pores of their skin
openings they never knew were there

Their tongues grow long
and wrap around the animal scent
as it scales the inside of skirts
Slippery into folds of fever fiery enough
that when the women walk away
Their ears are still steaming
like the extra hot latte coffee-of-the-day

MASQUERADES

The mother drops off the two girls at Starbucks
Seven-or-so-year olds pretending to be teenagers

Who totter on platform sandals
in low hung hip-huggers under bare midriffs

They buy their own caramel apple ciders
Peach polished nails curl around the cups
Pink lips leave kiss prints on the rims

And when the girls giggle
Paris Hilton hair exposes pierced ears
that play peek-a-boo with any onlooker

I order another decaf quad espresso
Watch like an undercover cop

To warrant that no customer
wears a business suit with a Barbie doll
and baby oil in his briefcase

Until the mother returns
Arms burdened with a Nordstrom bag

RELATIVELY SPEAKING

He intermittently reads *The New York Times*
idling in an overstuffed chair
Starbucks' recent attempt to cozy-up the place
So a person can pretend he's in his own living room
with a loving family on a Sunday morning

Today's family is another man
A stranger sitting in an adjacent chair
more than pleased to play the part
The reader says he's an attorney
between wives for the third time
All that alimony his new family member replies
Yeah well, the attorney knows the loopholes

The family one wishes he knew more ways
to get around his live-in mother-in-law
besides spending weekend mornings in coffee shops
His truck driving job solving the weekday dilemma

The attorney reads some personal ads out loud
Says he wouldn't hesitate to fly anywhere
in the world to bring back the right woman
But he'd leave her mother there

The truck driver admits he's never traveled out of the U. S.
Like Bush before he was president
Then wonders whether the dollar he put in the counter
donation box will wade its way through Southeast Asian
government graft to tsunami victims

The attorney was planning a trip to Thailand
but will probably postpone with all that mess over there
He mutters something about a tee-off time
Takes his last gulp of coffee from his grande cup
And returns *The Times* to the sales rack on his way out

SINGLE AT THE SECOND CUP COFFEE SHOP

He asks if I'm Carol
A serious man squeezing a paper coffee cup
and smelling like an ad for Calvin Klein cologne

My denial so devastatingly disappointing
that he dashes straight to his Porsche convertible
And in despair peels out of the parking lot

Or his expectation so exceedingly unmet
that he chauffeurs disillusion and any further gamble
to his wheels of fortune and spins out of the game

I don't even know the rules
But finish my iced Italian roast
Feeling like a woman who lied on her resume

WHERE THERE'S SMOKE

There's a World Cup Coffee man on a patio
Lips encircling a cigarette
in bad boy demeanor
Suckle love chiseling his cheekbones

And I inhale simultaneously
Sharp and shallow
Unlike him and his lazy draw
two tables away
Unaware of my ill-mannered stare
Of his smoke signals that send
seductive language to like kind

Silent alarms sounding
more than secondhand smoke
Flashbacks of Salem cigarettes
and other stale hungers burn fresh
And the saint of safety
is supplanted by devil-may-care

I wonder whether his hands
are as hazardous
as the come-hither nicotine
Whether the heat rising from my belly
is vicarious or lascivious

Either way I want to cut and run
Coffee half consumed
Leave the cravings commingled
with caffeine in the cup
Instead I stay spellbound
Die-hard held by old conflicts

➢

Caffeine combining with compulsion
And with questions like
Will I outlast his next light-up
Listen to life in long-term whispers
Or will I banish hazards to hell
And burn in the fire of gratification
Its short fuse a live-out-loud
shout of fortitude

STUCK IN THE WEB

A man wearing a cowboy hat
at the next table
stares through eyes blue as Montana Big Sky
A stalk of hair the color of ripened wheat
rebels against a ponytail
and rides over the slope of his ear

After a desire drought of months
I'm imagining harvest
and a slow dance to Willie Nelson
When he says *There's a half-price sticker*
on the sleeve of your shirt

A clear-day sunshine smile
crinkles infinity in his eyes
My hog-caller laugh
having little to do with the price of my blouse
bellows over the espresso machine thunder

As a woman carrying coffees walks up
to fence-in her cowboy with a barbed frown
And I go home to roam
the easier electronic open range

WHAT'S IN A NAME

He didn't come to Starbucks
for coffee yesterday or today
I listen for the tap-tap of his cane
The breath that sighs from the easy chair
next to mine as he sinks into it every morning
When I drag out my mental scrapbook
from a summer in Osaka to manage
Konnichewa or *Ohayo Gozaimasu*

He tries simple English
like the haiku he grew up with
Silent words sometimes shape our lips
His scowl when someone beats me to *my* chair
My smile at his vigilance

Mostly we rely on fingers
A tap on his shoulder before
I hand him a piece of chocolate
Curl of his pointer when his voice fails
and I lean in for his *Thank you*
A not-to-worry wave when he shuffles
to the restroom

I like this limited relationship
The almost romance of it
The quiet between us and the mystique
I worry and want to call him
now that I've finished my refill
But realize I don't even know his name

BLESSINGS

All of them at Starbucks on Thanksgiving morning
Solo men whose women don't exist
Or are home cooking in concert
with a country of women and a hick town of men

Surrounding families speaking German and Japanese
who will later eat turkey and cranberries
at someone else's house
Secretly wondering why the ballyhoo
The British couple trying not to think too hard
about pilgrims and revolutions
A man wearing an embroidered kufi

Yet why not an international day of gratitude
A day away from differences, right here now
Push tables together, carve up a pumpkin cake
Dress the morning in coffees from other countries
and celebration of the one we're in
Hold hands in a blessing that bars
bloodshed, politics and religion
Cheerio, ohayo, salam, dankbar

Just Deserts

I

Christmas Past wore its judge's robe
this Christmas Eve morning
Slammed down its Old Testament gavel
as it exacted sentence
for skipping school and Sunday ethics
The dress that stole its way from Buttrey's
into a red wrapped box for my mother
forty years ago on this very eve

Today the three avenging angels descended
from high school into Starbucks
and ascended with my purse
To hail everything unwanted
out of their car window
Leaving a Hansel and Gretel trail
to the nearest shopping center
To disperse the fifteen $100 bills
as though manna from heaven

The destination where I would have done the same
A leather jacket coveted by the husband
Sets of dishes for the daughters' first houses
Pinpricks compared to the gaping hole
left by the notebook of partial poems
One-of-a-kind family photos
And the airline gift card carried for five years
to hold onto love from a stepsister

➤

II

This violation, this small rape right in public
The boys wouldn't know how a woman's purse
is an appendage they'll never have
The ache of a missing limb that throbs with each
empty reach for lipstick or car keys
How the secrets we carry there are as sacred as a diary
Our real weight, the words from someone
as gone as his last cell phone message
Or the Valium that we need to get through the day

They may later learn of the holidays they stole
The peace of place and mind
Days flying around in circles
of change, cancel and replace
Instead of nesting and feeding the fold
They may even learn to care

Like the bicyclist who found a driver's license
beside the road and changed his course
The homeless man who took blank checks
to the bank without leaving the location
of the alleys where he sleeps
Starbucks' staff and customers
with coffees of compassion for the next week

Where Christmas carols still send
goodwill through the air
While a woman drinks decaf
and unravels the dark fabric of a dress
from a department store that long ago
filed for bankruptcy

YOU'VE COME A LONG WAY BABY

The scene in Edwardian England
was a smoke-filled room
with windows dimmed by steam
Rising around a busy woman
who brewed coffee over a blue-flamed stove

The all-male babble of voices
from clusters around small tables
Men engaged in card games or backgammon
Others expounding on politics of the day
Animating the air's heavy haze
as they exhaled from porcelain pipes

I was the Bohemian camouflaged
as a man in black corduroy knickers
alone in the corner
Breasts bandaged flat
And writing first drafts in margins
of the coffee shoppe's newsletter
My words for sale in a stack
of chapbooks beside me

Two pennies apiece
to support my coffee house habit
Or if requested
a tenor rendition of my latest verse
A sonnet, cinquain or rondelet
Always something in rhyme

➤

Airwaves in coffee cafés today sag
with the weight of cell phone conversations
satellite songs, colossal coffee machine growls
and a bisexual blend of voices
The only segregation cigarette determined
by smokers on patios

My voice and verse as free as my body
under mini-skirt, black tights and cowboy boots
The coffee is what comes costumed
as Café Mocha, Americana, Caramel Macchiato
or other equally indecipherable epithets
But the chapbooks still stack beside me
And a sale buys the day's quota of caffeine

Ellaraine Lockie is a widely published and awarded poet, nonfiction book author, and essayist. *Coffee House Confessions* is her tenth poetry chapbook. Her recent books have received the Best Individual Collection Award from *Purple Patch* magazine in England, the San Gabriel Poetry Festival Chapbook Prize, and *The Aurorean's* Chapbook Pick. She teaches poetry workshops and serves as Poetry Editor for the lifestyles magazine, *Lilipoh*. Ellaraine writes every morning in a coffee shop no matter where she is in the world.

Made in the USA
Middletown, DE
24 October 2022